The MAILBOX®

Beach

S0-BEF-204

THE BEST OF The MAILBOX® MAGAZINE

Our best beach activities and reproducibles from the 1997–2003 issues of *The Mailbox*® magazine

- **Literacy Ideas**

- **Math Activities**

- **Learning Centers**

- **Science Activities**

- **Songs, Poems, and Fingerplays**

- **Arts-and-Crafts Ideas**

And Much More!

Build Early Learning Skills!

Editorial Team: Becky S. Andrews, Kimberley Bruck, Karen P. Shelton, Diane Badden, Thad H. McLaurin, Sharon Murphy, Karen A. Brudnak, Juli Docimo Blair, Sarah Hamblet, Hope Rodgers, Dorothy C. McKinney

Production Team: Lori Z. Henry, Pam Crane, Rebecca Saunders, Jennifer Tipton Cappoen, Chris Curry, Sarah Foreman, Theresa Lewis Goode, Greg D. Rieves, Eliseo De Jesus Santos II, Barry Slate, Donna K. Teal, Zane Williard, Tazmen Carlisle, Marsha Heim, Lynette Dickerson, Mark Rainey

www.themailbox.com

Manufactured in the United States
10 9 8 7 6 5 4 3 2 1

Table of Contents

Thematic Units

A Day at the Beach 3
Bring a splash of fun to your classroom learning centers with these beach-themed ideas.

Sand and Surf Centers 6
Surf's up! Use these exciting center ideas to bring the beach to life for your little learners.

Simple Science 16
Have some summer fun while honing youngsters' observation skills with these super seashell activities.

More Ideas to Dive Into! 18

Build a variety of developmentally appropriate skills with even more beach-themed activities, center ideas, songs, arts-and-crafts ideas, classroom displays, and recipes.

Reproducible Practice Pages 45

Reinforce basic skills with fun, ready-to-use practice pages.

A Day At The Beach

Bring the sensations of the sun, the sand, and the sea to your classroom learning centers with these balmy ideas. Come on in—let's spend a day at the beach!

ideas by Carrie Lacher

Set a Maritime Mood

Wash away the winter blues and sparkle student interest when you transform your classroom into a seaside setting. Before your Beach Day, contact local travel agencies to ask for donations of travel posters featuring sunny beach locales. Display the posters on your classroom walls and windows. Next hang strips of blue and green crepe paper from your ceiling to give the feeling of ocean waves in motion. Add the warmth of sparkling sunshine by hanging strips of silver Mylar® or metallic ribbon. In the background, play some lively calypso music or a recording of the sounds of the surf (available from nature stores and some craft stores). Surf's up!

Sensory Area

Down in the Nitty-Gritty

A day at the beach means a day in the sand! Thrill little ones with an opportunity to feel sand between their fingers and toes at your beach-themed sensory area. In addition to your sand table, fill several large tubs or even a wading pool with sand; then thoroughly dampen the sand with water. Supply visitors with pails, scoopers, sand molds, and shells. To help keep the sand moist, place a small spritz bottle of water in the area. Encourage little ones to work cooperatively to build castles. For super sandy fun, invite children to remove their shoes and socks and wiggle their bare feet in the sand. Challenge them to draw designs with their toes. Keep a tub of warm water and beach towels nearby. What a scoop of ticklish fun!

Bathing Beauties

Something's fishy about this beachwear, but it's just what the weather calls for during your winter getaway! To make bathing "suits" for your dramatic play area, ask parents to donate children's old and used bathing suits (or check your thrift store for bargain beachwear). Purchase an adult-sized beige or brown T-shirt for each suit collected. Cut each bathing suit along the side and bottom seams. Pin the front and back of each suit to a shirt; then sew them in place. During your Beach Day, youngsters who dress in these bathing suits are sure to catch a wave of fun!

Debbie Hugli • Carousel Preschool • Downey, CA

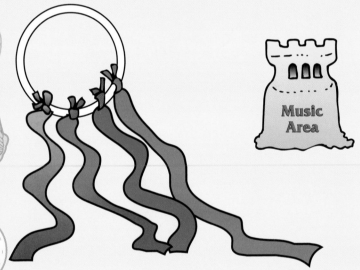

Swing and Sway

Bring a splash of colors to your music or listening area with these sparkling ocean streamers. To make a streamer, cut out the inside circle from a plastic margarine-tub lid. To the remaining plastic ring, tie lengths of blue, green, and metallic ribbon or cellophane. In this activity center, place recordings of gentle instrumental melodies or an ocean-related tune. Little ones will soon be afloat with maritime music and movement!

Constructing Castles...and Other Sandy Structures

A day at the beach would be incomplete without building a sand castle, so use this tip to add the texture of beach sand to your block area. Trace one side of each block (in a small set) onto sandpaper. Cut along the outline on the sandpaper; then use masking tape or clear-drying glue to adhere each sandpaper shape to its matching block. Add a pail of shells to the center. Invite your youngsters to build sand structures using the blocks and the shells. Watch out for that...WAVE!

Scented Seaside Play Dough

Play Dough Center

Place this supersmooth, sea-sparkly play dough in a center along with seashells and nautical-themed cookie cutters. Your classroom will soon be awash with the scents of the seashore!

3 cups flour
1.5 ounces cream of tartar
¾ cup salt
3 tablespoons cooking oil
3 cups water
1 tablespoon coconut extract
yellow food coloring
gold glitter

ombine the first five ingredients in a large pot. Whisk together until free
lumps. Stir in the coconut extract and yellow food coloring. Stir the
ixture constantly over medium heat until it pulls away from the sides of
e pot and forms a large ball. Knead the ball on a lightly floured board
ntil the dough is silky smooth. Knead in the desired amount of gold glit-
r. When the mixture has cooled, store it in an airtight container.

Tanika

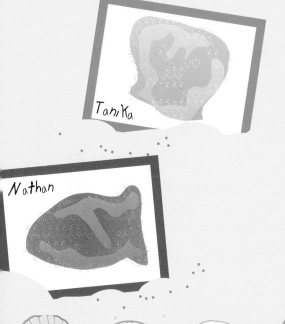

Nathan

"Sand-sational" Painting

Painting Center

Add this nautical concoction to your painting center, and it's sure to get plenty of beach exposure. To make the paint, thoroughly mix together one part flour with two parts salt. Slowly add liquid tempera paint in equal proportion to the salt-flour mixture. Stir the mixture until it is lump-free and the consistency of thick cake batter. Pour this mixture into paint cups and place them in your painting center. Provide tagboard or recycled cardboard for use as canvases with this seashore paint. Encourage each painter to spread a thick layer of paint onto his canvas. Allow the completed paintings to dry for several days. Youngsters will be dazzled by the magic of the salty paints—a seaside sparkle in every picture!

Sand and Surf Centers

You just might hear the roar of the ocean when you set up centers that make learning as exciting as a day at the beach!

ideas contributed by LeeAnn Collins
Sunshine House Preschool, Lansing, MI

Discovery Center
A Little Bit of Beach in a Bag

How do you bring a bit of beach right into your classroom? It's easy! Gather a few seashells, some resealable plastic bags, and sand. Partially fill each bag with sand; then add a few seashells to each bag. Seal the bags with clear packaging tape and then place them at your discovery center. Have each child tilt the bags back and forth, and observe the movement of the sand and shells. For added sensory discovery, encourage youngsters to listen carefully to the sound of the moving sand. Hey, that sounds a lot like the ocean!

Sarah Booth, Messiah Nursery School South Williamsport, PA

Literacy Center
S Is for Sand

Sand pails aren't just for building sand castles! Fill one with magnetic letters to help build youngsters' literacy skills! In advance, photocopy the cards on pages 12 and 13. Color the cards. Laminate them and cut them out. Next, place a self-adhesive magnetic strip on the back of each card. Set the cards near a magnetic board and the pail filled with letters. To use the center, a child places a card on the board, finds the matching magnetic letters, and then places them under the card to spell the word.

Five Little Sand Castles

To prepare for this center, record yourself reciting the poem below and then place the recording near your flannelboard. Use the patterns on page 14 to make five felt sand castle cutouts; then place the sand castles on the flannelboard. To use the center, a child begins playing the recording and removing the castles according to the poem. When students are familiar with this activity, encourage them to recite the poem without the recording.

Five little sand castles built by the shore.
Along came a wave and whoosh!
There were four.

Four little sand castles built just for me.
Along came a wave and whoosh!
There were three.

Three little sand castles built just for you.
Along came a wave and whoosh!
There were two.

Two little sand castles built in the sun.
Along came a wave and whoosh!
There was one.

One little sand castle built just for fun.
Along came a wave and whoosh!
There were none.

Art Center

Sturdy Sand Castles

Having your sand castle washed away sure can be a disappointment! With this craft idea, your youngsters can create sand castles that are here to stay! To make a castle, provide a child with paper towel tubes cut into a variety of lengths. Help the child use a paintbrush to cover each tube with glue. (To keep the glue off little fingers, clip a spring-type clothespin to the tube and have the child hold the tube by the clothespin.) Next, roll the tube in a shallow pan of sand until it is covered. Set the tubes aside to dry. Afterward, help the child create a sand castle by gluing the sides of the tubes together with craft glue. Next, pour Elmer's glue onto a small plastic plate so that the bottom of the plate is covered. Set the castle on the plate. Sprinkle sand over the glue; then pour off any excess sand. For a finishing touch, invite the child to glue a construction paper flag to the top of one of the tubes. Ah, a sand castle fit for a queen!

7

Calling All Sand Fans!

Invite your little ones to dig in to some grainy fun by placing a batch of sand dough in your play dough area. To make a batch of sandy dough, follow the recipe shown. Place the dough in an airtight container and set it near a bucket of small shells. Invite each child to roll out the dough and then press the shells into it to make impressions. Or have students use the shells and dough to create some sensational sand castles.

Sandy Play Dough

Ingredients:
1 c. flour
½ c. salt
1 tbsp. cream of tartar
1 c. water
¼ c. sand
brown food coloring paste

Mix all of the ingredients together in a medium-sized pot. Stir constantly over medium heat until the mixture is slightly lumpy. Turn out onto a piece of foil and let cool; then knead until smooth.

Jill Simon
Poland Boardman Child Care Center
Poland, OH

Weaving for Wee Ones

Beach chairs are great for relaxing at the shore. But did you know they also make wonderful weaving tools? Invite your preschoolers to participate in some weaving fun with this center idea. In advance, gather a couple of beach chairs similar to the one shown. Tie lengths of ribbon to each chair; then have your youngsters weave the ribbons through the chairs. Over, under, over, under...

Math Center
Sand Pails and Shovels

To prepare for this math center, make ten copies of the pail and shovel patterns on page 15. Color the patterns and then program each pail with a different number from 1 to 10. Program each shovel with a different set of stickers from 1 to 10. Laminate the pails and shovels; then use a craft knife to cut a three-inch slit across the top of each pail. Place the shovels and pails in the center. To complete the activity, a child reads the numeral on each pail and finds the shovel with the matching set of stickers. Then he places the shovel inside the pail by slipping it through the slit. To reinforce other preschool skills, program the pails and shovels with other pairs for youngsters to match.

Snack Center
Seashore Snack

Set up this snack center and invite your tots to ake a dip—in some edible sand! Read through e recipe shown and then gather the needed gredients and supplies. Have each child follow e steps to create a fun fruit dip that will remind er of the beach!

gredients needed to make one snack:
tbsp. instant vanilla pudding mix
c. milk
rumbled vanilla wafers
–4 apple slices
upplies:
oz. paper cup for each child
blespoon
c. measuring cup
astic spoon for each child

Place pudding mix and milk in a paper cup and en mix thoroughly with the plastic spoon. Top e pudding with vanilla wafer crumbs. Dip apple ices in the mixture and eat!

Blocks Area
Perimeter and Area for Preschoolers?

It's true! You can introduce your youngsters to the concepts of perimeter and area in a perfectly preschool way! Place a variety of beach towels in your blocks area. Invite each child to lay out a towel and then place blocks around the outside edges of the towel (perimeter). Or have her use the blocks to cover the entire towel (area). Encourage the child to count the number of blocks needed to cover the perimeter or area of the towel. Then have her remove the blocks and try the activity again with a different towel.

Flip-Flop Fun
Here's a painting idea your preschoolers will flip for! In advance, collect a variety of old child-sized flip-flops. Place them at your painting center near shallow pans of paint. Invite each child to dip the sole of a flip-flop into the paint and then press it on a sheet of paper to make prints.

Sand Writing
Take a break from conventional writing tools with this sandy writing center. Cover the inside of a large shoebox lid with dark-colored Con-Tact paper. Then pour enough sand into the lid to cover the bottom of it. Set the lid at your writing center along with copies of the picture cards on pages 12 and 13. To use the center, a child chooses a card and then uses his finger to write the word in the sand. To erase the writing, he simply tilts the box until the word disappears. Now the sandy tablet is ready for another round of writing!

Shell Search
Don't you just love finding that perfect shell on the beach? Your youngsters will experience that same excitement when you set up this shell search at your sand table. In advance, hide a supply of shells in your sand table. (Check your local craft store for prepackaged shells.) Place sifters and sand shovels near the table; then let the search begin! For an added challenge, have youngsters sort the shells after finding them. Wow! Look at this shell!

Beach Blanket Bingo

Use the picture cards on pages 12 and 13 to make a set of lotto gameboards for this center. To begin, make several copies of the pictures. Cut them apart and then glue them onto pieces of tagboard to create different gameboards. Provide each child in the center with a board and a handful of shells to use as markers. Then give students verbal cues, such as "You use this after you've been in the water." Have each child find the correct pictures on his gameboard and mark each one with a shell. The game ends when a child has marked all the pictures on his board. Bingo!

Reading Area

Seaside Reading

There's nothing more relaxing than reading a good book on the shore of the beach. So transform your reading area into a pretend beach, and your little ones might want to read the day away! First, arrange child-sized beach chairs in the area. Then fill several beach bags with sunglasses, empty bottles of suntan lotion, and a supply of summer reading material. Play a recording of ocean sounds in the area. Then invite students to grab a bag, slather on some lotion, don the glasses, and read!

Picture Cards

Use with "S Is for Sand" on page 6, "Sand Writing" on page 10, and "Beach Blanket Bingo" on page 11.

sand

TEC61054

shell

TEC61054

pail

TEC61054

crab

TEC61054

towel

TEC61054

sun

TEC61054

Picture Cards

Use with "S Is for Sand" on page 6, "Sand Writing" on page 10, and "Beach Blanket Bingo" on page 11.

ball

TEC61054

fish

TEC61054

hat

TEC61054

bird

TEC61054

kite

TEC61054

cap

TEC61054

Sand Castle Patterns

Use with "Five Little Sand Castles" on page 7.

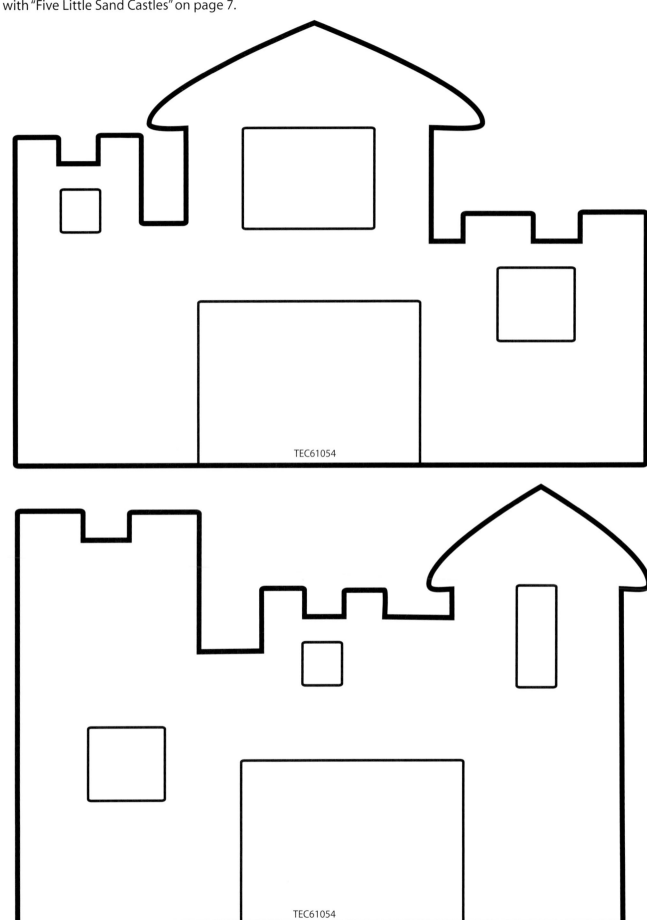

TEC61054

TEC61054

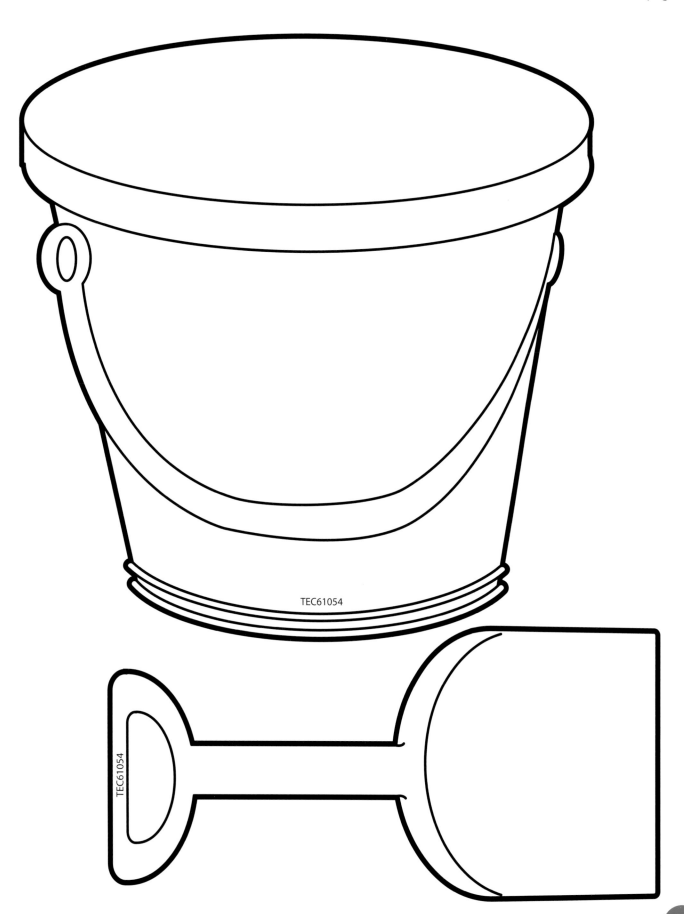

TEC61054

TEC61054

Seashell Sensations

Dive into observation skills with these super seashell activities.

ideas by Suzanne Moore

The Shape of Shells

Start your seashell study with a small-group **sensory** activity that is cloaked in mystery. Before students arrive for the day, scatter several shells on the floor and then cover them with a large beach towel. Invite a small group of students to the area and explain that you have hidden mystery objects under the towel. Invite each child to feel one of the objects through the towel. Encourage students to describe what they feel and then guess what is under the towel. After each child has made a guess, remove the towel to reveal the shells. Have students closely examine the shells and then discuss their observations.

DID YOU KNOW?
Every seashell was once the home of a sea animal.

Shell Centers

Continue to sharpen students' **observation skills** with these easy-to-create centers.

- Stock an area with a basket of small shells and several copies of the sorting sheet on page 17. Direct students to sort the shells onto the sheet by appearance.
- Place several shells near a supply of play dough and invite each child to make impressions of the shells in the dough.
- Stock an area with a supply of shells, hand lenses, paper, and crayons. Encourage each child to use the lenses to closely examine the shells. Then direct her to use the crayons and paper to trace the shells and make rubbings.
- Place some shells near a balance scale and a supply of counting blocks. Invite students to use the scale and blocks to weigh the shells.

Shell Sorting

Note to the teacher: Use with "Shell Centers" on page 16.

Beach Ball Blast

Have some summer fun while reviewing the **alphabet**. Use a permanent marker to divide a beach ball into 26 sections. Write a different letter in each section. Teach your youngsters the chant at the right. Then arrange students in a circle. After reciting the chant, call out a child's name and toss the ball into the air. Encourage that child to catch the ball, look at the section that his right pointer finger is touching, and then name the letter. Have him toss the ball back to you, and begin the chant again. Continue until each child has had a turn. Ready…catch!

adapted from an idea by Deb Scala
Mt. Tabor School
Mt. Tabor, NJ

Listen closely as I name
One of you to play this game.
I'll toss the ball up in the sky.
You can catch it if you try!

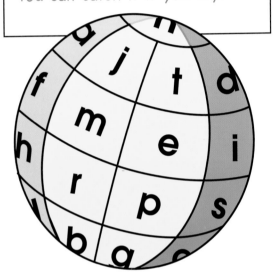

ABC Octopus

Need a helping hand at circle time? Use this idea and you'll have eight hands to help with **letter recognition**! Use the patterns on pages 37 and 38 to cut an octopus body and arms to form an octopus on the flannelboard. Next, obtain a set of foam alphabet letters. Attach a piece of self-adhesive Velcro to the back of each letter and to each arm of the octopus. Place the letters in a container near the octopus. During your group time, have eight children each choose a different letter to place on the octopus. Then have the class identify the letters. For more literacy fun, encourage your youngsters to name words that begin with the letters, make the letter sounds, or find the letters in their names.

Tami Bertini
Bondurant-Farrar Community Schools
Bondurant, IA

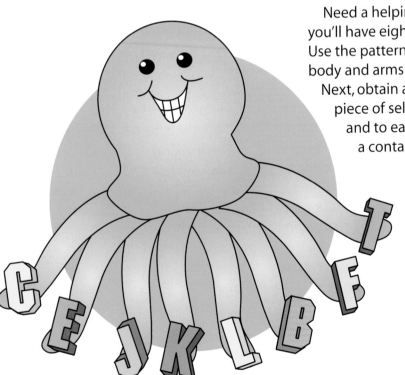

Dive Into!

Seashell Hunt

Collecting shells is a time-honored tradition at the beach. And when your students collect these shells, they'll also be collecting **letter recognition** skills. To prepare, duplicate the shell patterns on page 39 to make as many shells as you desire. Then label each shell with a letter. Cut the shells apart and scatter them in your classroom. Set out plastic sand pails, each labeled with a different letter. Then invite students to hunt for shells and deposit each one in the pail with the corresponding letter.

Shell Game

A hidden hermit crab will keep youngsters guessing in this **alphabet** game. To prepare, use the patterns on page 39 to make 12 shells and one copy of the hermit crab. Write a different letter on each shell; then place the shells in a grid in a pocket chart, three across and four down. Tuck the hermit crab pattern behind one of the shells. To play the game, one child at a time calls out one of the letters. Lift the corresponding shell to see if the hermit crab is hiding behind that letter. The child who finds the hidden hermit crab is the winner! When you're ready to play again, simply change the hermit crab's hiding place.

adapted from an idea by Diana Phillips
Murrayville-Woodson School
Murrayville, IL

Written in the Sand

Welcome barefoot season as you reinforce **beginning writing skills**. Purchase a decorative hole puncher that punches the shape of a foot. (These punches are often found in the scrapbooking sections of most department stores.) Encourage each child to use the punch to make a supply of feet from tan or brown construction paper. Have each child create a beach scene on a large sheet of construction paper. Then help her to glue her feet onto the lower portion of the paper to create her name or a summer-related word. Display the projects together on a bulletin board and help youngsters read each word.

adapted from an idea by Barbara Meyer
Lincoln Elementary School
Dayton, KY

Sand Pail Surprise

What's the scoop on this **language development** activity for your outdoor sandbox? It encourages hand-eye coordination! Bury a number of plastic bugs in sand pails. Invite a little beachcomber to use a small shovel to scoop the bugs from a pail while singing the song to the right. When each child finishes, have him refill his pail with sand and bugs for the next child.

There's a Bug at the Bottom of My Pail
(sung to the tune of "There's a Hole at the Bottom of the Sea")

There's a bug at the bottom of my pail.
There's a bug at the bottom of my pail.
Scoop it out! Scoop it out!
Scoop it out from the bottom of my pail.

Patricia Moeser
U. W. Preschool Lab Site One
Madison, WI

Sing "Twinkle, Twinkle, Little Star."

Go Fish for a Wish

Promote children's **language skills** by inviting your students to choose activities for circle time. Make a supply of fish cutouts (pattern on page 40). Ask each child to dictate a circle-time wish; then write her response on a fish. For example, a child might say, "I wish we could sing 'Twinkle, Twinkle, Little Star,' " or "I wish we could play Duck, Duck, Goose." Collect these fishy wishes and keep them in a fishbowl in your group area. Each day at group time, invite a child to fish for a wish. Have her draw out one fish; then read and grant the wish! When the bowl is empty, restock it with more requests!

Ada Goren, Winston-Salem, NC

Pin the Arms on the Octopus

This **counting** adaptation of Pin the Tail on the Donkey is eight times as much fun! To prepare, cut out a construction paper copy of the octopus body on page 37 and two construction paper copies of the arm patterns on page 38. Tape the octopus body on a wall in your classroom; then place loops of masking tape on the back of each arm. Provide eight children each with an octopus arm. Help one child at a time play Pin the Arms on the Octopus. After each turn, lead youngsters in counting the arms on the octopus.

Patricia Merrick
T. G. Connors Elementary
Hoboken, NJ

Seashore Skills

Youngsters will enjoy practicing **basic math skills** if they can do it by the shore. Using bulletin board paper, create a simple scene similar to the one shown. (Use the patterns on pages 40 and 41.) Place the scene on the floor, set the youngsters around it, and dive into circle time with the activities listed below.

- Show a numeral card and ask a volunteer to place the corresponding number of cutouts on the scene.
- Group the cutouts in sets of one to five. Have students count aloud as a volunteer practices one-to-one correspondence by pointing to all of one type of cutout.
- Place a collection of cutouts on the scene. Describe one cutout for a volunteer to find and take away.

Pirate's Treasure

Ahoy, matey! Send your petite pirates on a quest for buried treasure in your **sand table**! Bury various pieces of costume jewelry in the sand; then place a toy treasure chest (or box decorated to look like one) nearby. Encourage youngsters to use their hands and toy shovels to dig up the treasure and add it to the chest. At the end of center time, ask them to bury the loot again for other pirates to find!

Carol Breeding
New Life Center Daycare
Des Moines, IA

Ocean in Motion

Children will daydream about splashing in the surf as they manipulate this ocean in a bottle. For this **discovery** activity, remove the label from an empty, two liter plastic soda bottle; then rinse the bottle well. Fill one-fourth of the bottle with sand. Fill the rest of the bottle with water; then add a drop or two of blue food coloring. Complete the bottle scene by adding small seashells and other plastic ocean trinkets. Hot-glue the cap onto the bottle. Encourage students to shake, turn, and roll the bottle to explore its contents.

Jill Benner and Tammy Strayer
GLEE Nursery School
Mechanicsburg, PA

Classroom Ocean

Can't take your preschoolers to the ocean? Then bring the ocean to your preschoolers with this **discovery** center. Set up a small plastic wading pool in your discovery area. Cover the bottom of the pool with sand; then add water. Put in a variety of shells, as well as plastic or vinyl sea creatures and some toy boats. Have students wear plastic smocks as they play and explore in this miniature ocean!

Maegen Johnson
Keene Adventist Elementary
Keene, TX

Hold the Ocean in Your Hand!

Studying the ocean? Then this **discovery** project is perfect! Pour about a half inch of sand into the bottom of a plastic bag; then add a few shells. Next, mix up four batches of Knox clear gelatin according to the package instructions, using water as your liquid. (Do not use sweetened blue gelatin.) Add a few drops of blue food coloring. Gently pour the blue-tinted gelatin over the sand and shells. Slip a few plastic fish or other sea creatures into the gelatin; then put the container in the refrigerator. Once the gelatin is firm, remove the miniature ocean scene from the refrigerator, hold it in your hand, and look right through the "water"!

Sandie Ayers
Chesterbrook Academy
Sterling, VA

A Beautiful Day at the Beach

Have each child bring in a favorite beach towel to make this **movement** activity seem more like a real day at the beach! Ask everyone to spread his towel in a large open area. Then say, "It's a beautiful day at the beach. Let's go swimming!" Have children pantomime running into the waves and swimming through the water. Then invite them to head back to their towels to take a rest. Next, say, "It's a beautiful day at the beach. Let's go fishing!" Have students stand up, bait their hooks, and cast their imaginary fishing lines out into the water. Of course, everyone will catch a giant fish and struggle to reel it in! After they take another rest on their beach towels, make more suggestions for beach activities, such as jogging, surfing, or playing ball!

Ada Goren
Winston-Salem, NC

On the Water

Transform your **dramatic-play** center into a water wonderland! Set up a small inflatable boat and then add life jackets, plastic oars, toy fishing poles, inflatable beach toys, and beach towels. Encourage youngsters to role-play boating, fishing, swimming, and other water activities. What a perfect opportunity to help your little ones learn about water safety too!

Shelly Fales
Whittemore-Prescott Early Childhood Center
Whittemore, MI

At the Beach

At the beach,
The sun shines down.

I see smiles
On kids all around.

Smiling kids in the sand,

Smiling kids in the sea.

But the happiest kid
At the beach is me!

Patricia A. McMillan, Longwood, FL

25

A Song for the Seashore

Did you know that a trip to the beach can be a stimulating experience for all five senses? This song will help your youngsters remember just how "sense-ational" the seashore is!

*(sung to the tune of
"Do Your Ears Hang Low?")*

Feel sand in my toes.
Smell the ocean with my nose.
See the children splash and play
On a hot summer day.
Hear the ocean waves go ROAR
As they crash into the shore.
Taste the salty sea.

Karen Briggs
Marlborough Early Childhood Center
Marlborough, MA

So Long, Seagulls!

Don't you just love watching seagulls take flight at the beach? Sing this song and invite your little ones to fly like a seagull!

*(sung to the tune of
"Down by the Station")*

Down by the seashore
Early in the morning
See the flock of seagulls
All in a row.
See them flap their wings
And fly off toward the ocean.
Flap! Flap! Caw! Caw!
Off they go!

A Seaside Pail

Your youngsters will really dig this beach-themed art project! Gather the materials listed below; then help each child follow the directions. Once the pails are finished, display them with a shovel cutout on a bulletin board titled "We Dig Preschool!"

Materials needed for one pail:
light blue construction paper pail shape (approximately 7 1/2" x 10")
1" x 12" construction paper strip
tan crayon
shallow pans, each containing a thin layer of paint
sea creature-shaped sponges
marker
stapler

Directions:
1. Use a tan crayon to color the bottom of the pail to resemble sand.
2. Fold the pail in half lengthwise; then unfold it.
3. Dip a shaped sponge in paint and then make a print on one half of the pail. Repeat with the second sponge on the same half of the pail cutout.
4. Fold the pail, using your hand to smooth over the paper's surface to transfer the paint print to the opposite side. Unfold the pail.
5. After the paint is dry, use a marker to draw facial features on each sea creature.
6. Staple a paper strip to each side of the pail top to make a handle.

Judy Kelley
Lilja School
Natick, MA

Colored Sand

Make your own colored sand to use for summer art projects. In a plastic container, add four or five drops of food coloring to a cup of sand. Add two tablespoons of vinegar and enough water to make the sand mushy but not watery. Stir and then spread the wet sand onto a cookie sheet and allow it to dry in the sun for a few hours, or bake the sand in a low-temperature oven for an hour or two until dry.

Laura J. Michelon
Vineland Nazarene Learning Center
Vineland, NJ

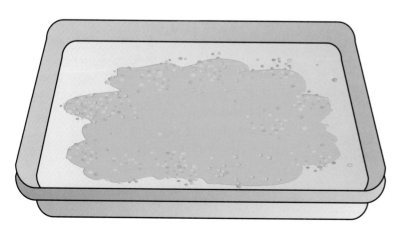

Sand Bottles

To prepare, purchase a bag of playground sand at your local home improvement store. Pour the sand into bowls or sand pails; then stir a different color of powdered tempera paint into each container. Working with two or three children at a time, give each child a funnel and a small clean plastic bottle with the label removed. Invite a child to spoon as much sand of each color as he desires into his bottle (through the funnel), creating colorful layers. When the bottle is full, secure the top with hot glue and admire the finished product!

Ann Becker
Deerwood Center
Milwaukee, WI

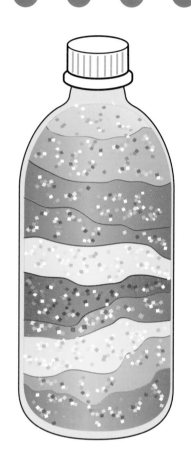

Grand Sand Containers

Prior to making this craft, collect an empty two-liter soda bottle and an empty three-liter soda bottle for each child. Use a craft knife to cut the tops off each container. Place each two-liter bottle inside a separate three-liter bottle and trim the tops so they are the same height. Next, mix play sand with powdered tempera paint to create batches of colored sand.

To make a sand container, have a child use a funnel to pour layers of colored sand in between the two bottles as shown. Be sure to hold the two-liter bottle in place as the child pours the sand. When the sand is approximately ¼ inch from the top, use a tube of caulk or grout to seal the sand in between the two bottles. This colorful craft is perfect for holding a bouquet of fresh flowers!

Robin Millar
Medford Lakes, NJ

Watercolor Sunset

There's nothing like a spectacular sunset at the beach! Invite each of your preschoolers to make her own version of this summer scene with watercolor paints. First, have her use a spray bottle to dampen a sheet of white construction paper with water. Then have her use watercolors to paint bands of colors across the paper. Hold the paper by the top corners over a tray, allowing the paint to drip and the colors to blend together. When the paint is dry, have the child glue a half circle cut from fluorescent orange paper near the bottom of the scene. Finally, help her glue on a torn strip of blue paper to simulate the ocean's waves. Beautiful!

Nancy O'Toole
Ready Set Grow
Grand Rapids, MN

Stunning Starfish

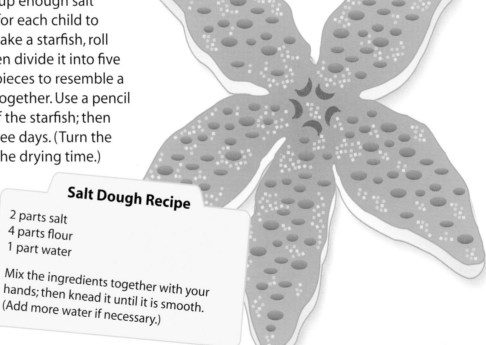

Captivate your little beachcombers with these pretty starfish. In advance, mix up enough salt dough (see the recipe shown) for each child to have a lime-sized portion. To make a starfish, roll the dough into a long rope; then divide it into five equal pieces. Arrange the five pieces to resemble a starfish; then press the center together. Use a pencil to add texture to the surface of the starfish; then set it aside to dry for two to three days. (Turn the starfish over midway through the drying time.) Finally, paint the dry starfish with a light coat of coral-colored tempera paint. Then sprinkle kosher salt on top of the wet paint. Display these starfish along a long strip of child-made ocean.

Salt Dough Recipe

2 parts salt
4 parts flour
1 part water

Mix the ingredients together with your hands; then knead it until it is smooth. (Add more water if necessary.)

Christine Guanipa
Covenant School
Arlington, MA

29

Sparkly Fish

Wait 'til you "sea" these fanciful fish! To make one, cut a simple fish shape from brightly colored construction paper; then cut out the center portion as shown. Next, squirt some glitter glue onto the center of a piece of waxed paper slightly larger than the fish shape. Use a paintbrush to spread the glue with short strokes, making the design resemble fish scales. When the glue is dry, trim the waxed paper and then glue or tape it behind the opening in the fish cutout. Add a dot eye and a friendly fishy smile, and this project is ready to display!

Barb Stefaniuk
Kerrobert Tiny Tots Playschool
Kerrobert, Saskatchewan, Canada

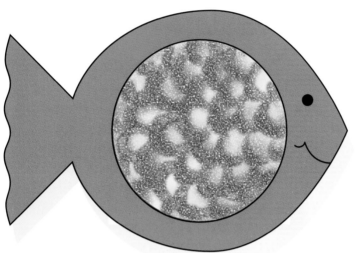

Glittery Goldfish

Transform your classroom into a giant fishbowl when you suspend these giant goldfish from the ceiling! To prepare, make a large, simple goldfish pattern (about two feet long) from tagboard. For each child, staple two 2' x 2' sheets of newsprint together. Help the child trace the goldfish pattern onto the newsprint and cut it out through both thicknesses of paper. Have the child paint both cutouts with orange tempera paint and then sprinkle gold glitter over the wet paint. When the paint is dry, have her add a sticker-dot eye. Then place the cutouts back-to-back and staple around the edges. If desired, leave an opening and stuff the fish lightly with tissue paper before stapling it shut. Your goldfish are ready to swim!

Eva Bareis
Westside Preschool
Rapid City, SD

Beach Props

Is there a beach in your classroom at this time of year? Enhance children's imaginary play by making simple sunglasses from craft foam! Use the sunglasses patterns on page 42 to make tagboard tracers. Then use the tracers to create craft foam glasses. Punch holes in the top corners of the glasses. Then twist a length of pipe cleaner through each hole to create an earpiece. Glue colored cellophane over the eyeholes to make the glasses more realistic. Invite each child to choose a pair of glasses and then decorate them with slick or puffy fabric paint. They'll look just "beach-y"!

Nancy Wolfgram
Kindercare Learning Center #1111
Lincoln, NE

"Gel-lyfish"

This peekaboo project is perfect to enhance a study of ocean critters! For each child, fold a sheet of construction paper in half. Draw three curved lines as shown. Have the child cut along the lines and discard the scraps. Then ask her to draw two eyes above the center cutout. Next, help her squirt a bit of clear hair gel into a zippered plastic bag. Then have her sprinkle in some glitter and metallic confetti. Squeeze out any air and seal the plastic bag. Tape the bag inside the jellyfish cutout so that the seal is covered by the paper. Then staple around the edges of the paper. Finally, have the child tape a few lengths of crepe paper streamer to the bottom of the jellyfish to create tentacles.

Karen Reed
Trailside Daycare
East Providence, RI

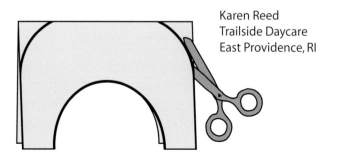

31

Highlight your youngsters with this starfish-studded display. Have each child glue sand on a separate yellow, orange, or pink starfish cutout (pattern on page 43). Later, hot-glue a photo of each child to the center of her starfish. For a watery effect, cover a background with crumpled blue bulletin-board paper. Mount the completed starfish, name labels, and a starfish character along with a title to complete this star-quality display.

Looking at this display, you can almost hear the sound of the ocean waves! Have each child decorate a paper swimsuit and then glue it onto a body cutout (pattern on page 44). Direct the child to draw facial features on the cutout to resemble herself; then invite her to add cutout snorkeling gear, floaters, or other beach accessories. Mount the cutouts on a sand and surf scene; then add other details to the display, such as umbrellas, towels, and little footprints in the sand!

Audrey Englehardt, Meadowbrook Elementary, Moro, IL

Sandy Sandwiches

Invite your little ones to help you make these sandwiches with just a bit of crunchy sand (toasted wheat germ). To make one, use a cookie cutter to cut a shell shape from a slice of whole wheat bread. Squeeze some honey onto this shape; then sprinkle it with the "sand." Get ready to crunch!

Magical Mermaid Potion

In advance, fill several ice-cube trays with water; then squirt a drop of blue food coloring into each cube. Put the trays in the freezer. Ask your class to help as you use warm water to prepare a pitcher of powdered lemonade-flavored drink. Have students take turns pouring one 12-ounce can of lemon-lime soda into the lemonade. Add about eight drops of yellow food coloring. For each child, pour a serving of this drink into a clear plastic cup. Then invite each child to drop one or two blue ice cubes into his yellow potion and stir it with a tropical straw. Watch the mermaid magic happen!

KIDS IN THE KITCHEN

Here's what to do:
- Collect the necessary ingredients and utensils using the lists on the recipe cards below.
- Photocopy the step-by-step recipe cards on page 35 or 36.
- Color the cards then cut them out.
- Follow the teacher preparation guidelines for that activity.

Beach in a Peach

Ingredients for one:
canned peach half
vanilla yogurt
graham cracker crumbs

Utensils and supplies:
3 serving bowls
3 serving spoons
paper bowl for each child
plastic spoon for each child
toothpick umbrella for each child

Teacher preparation:
For safety, use scissors to cut off the pointed tips of the toothpicks. Arrange the ingredients and utensils near the step-by-step recipe cards (see page 35).

Tuna Toast

Ingredients for one:
slice of bread, toasted
1 tbsp. tuna salad
black olive slice

Utensils and supplies:
fish-shaped cookie cutter
tablespoon
paper plate for each child
toaster *(for teacher use only)*

Teacher preparation:
Prepare a batch of tuna salad. Toast a slice of bread for each child. Arrange the ingredients and utensils near the step-by-step recipe cards (see page 36).

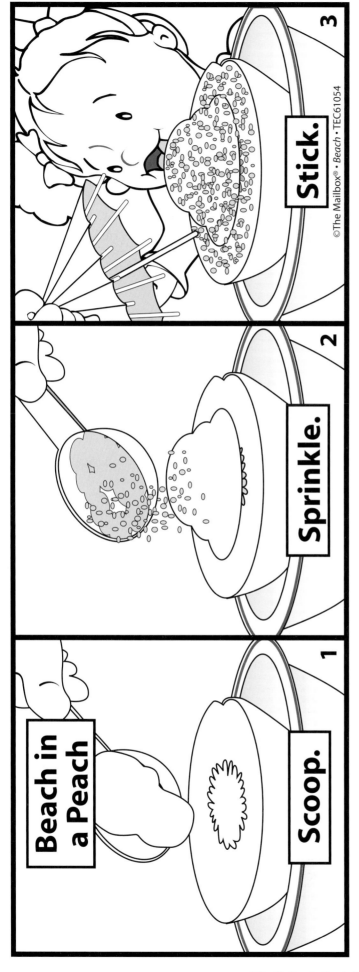

Beach in a Peach

Scoop.

©The Mailbox® • *Beach* • TEC61054

Sprinkle.

Stick.

©The Mailbox® • *Beach* • TEC61054

Recipe Cards

Use with "Tuna Toast" on page 34.

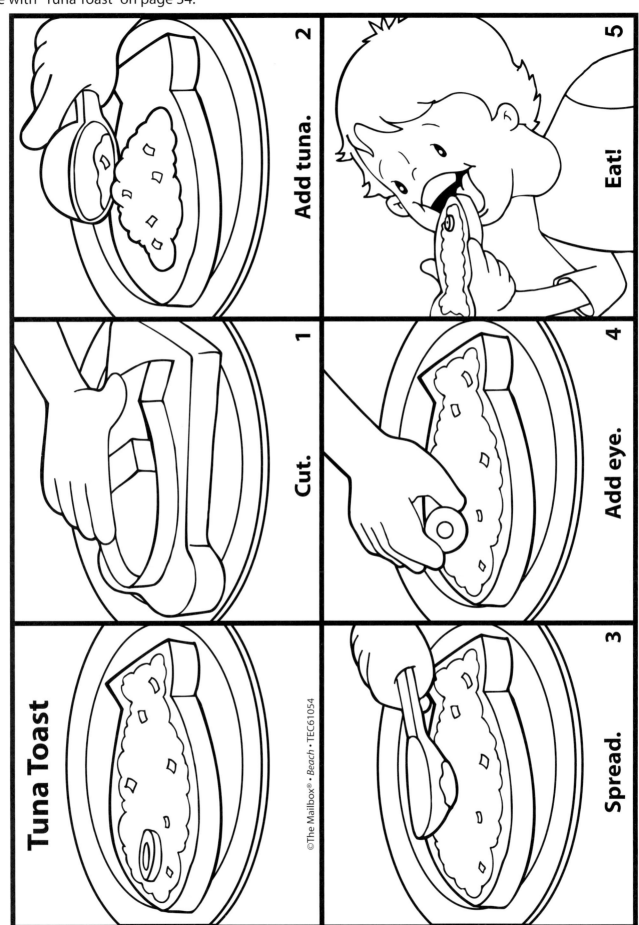

2 Add tuna.

5 Eat!

1 Cut.

4 Add eye.

Tuna Toast

3 Spread.

©The Mailbox® • *Beach* • TEC61054

TEC61054

Octopus Arm Patterns

Use with "ABC Octopus" on page 18 and "Pin the Arms on the Octopus" on page 21.

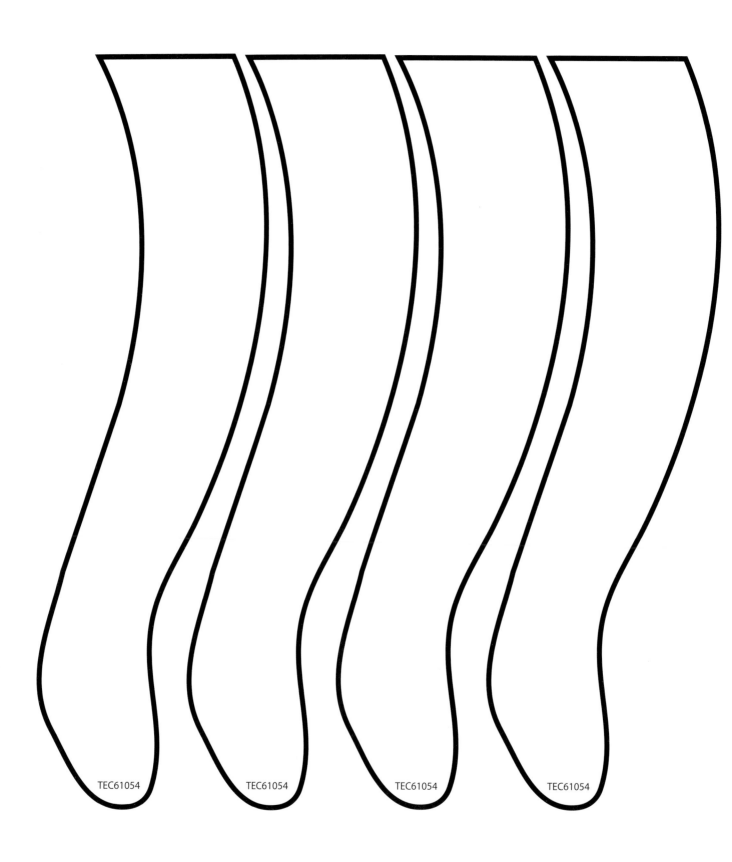

TEC61054

TEC61054

TEC61054

TEC61054

Use with "Seashell Hunt" and "Shell Game" on page 19.

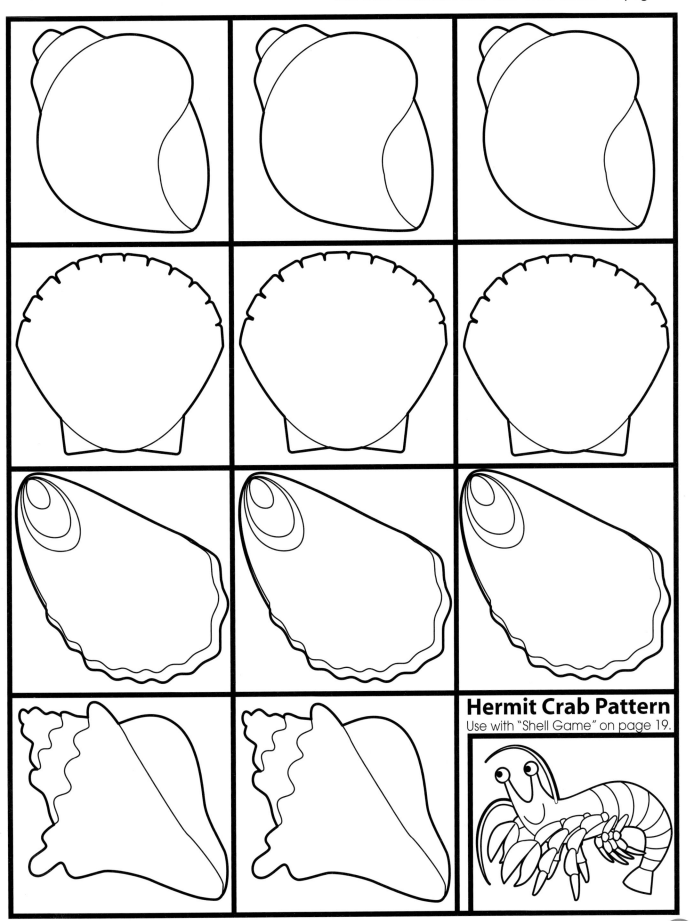

Hermit Crab Pattern
Use with "Shell Game" on page 19.

Fish Patterns

Use with "Go Fish for a Wish" on page 20
and "Seashore Skills" on page 21.

TEC61054

TEC61054

TEC61054

Sunglasses Patterns
Use with "Beach Props" on page 31.

TEC61054

TEC61054

TEC61054

TEC61054

Body Pattern
Use with "Ready for the Beach!" on page 32.

Underwater Wonders

Color 2  orange.

Color 3 purple.

Color 1 yellow.

Beach Patrol

Color the summer picture in each box.

Name_____

Shell Sort

 Cut. Glue to match the letters.

A B

C D

A B C D

Name _____

Pick a Pail

 Cut.

Glue to match the beginning sound.

©The Mailbox® • *Beach* • TEC61054